SEA OTTER

Jane and Paul Annixter

SEA OTTER

illustrated by John Hamberger

HOLIDAY HOUSE, INC.   NEW YORK

By the same authors

THE RUNNER

BUFFALO CHIEF

HORNS OF PLENTY

WINDIGO

WAGON SCOUT

THE GREAT WHITE

VIKAN THE MIGHTY

AHMEEK

WHITE SHELL HORSE

For Amanda and John

CONTENTS

SEA OTTER

Lutra

The little cove on the rocky island shore backed by high cliffs looked safe to the sea otters. It was located on one of the larger islands off the south coast of Alaska, ordinarily avoided by the harried and hunted band. But this day they were tired from a stormy ocean passage and needed rest.

Not that sea otters minded stormy weather. They sported in the heaviest seas, riding the crests of the waves, careening into the troughs. After enough of this they might descend to the untroubled depths and swim fishwise for a while. Though air-breathing mammals, their oxygen-rich blood allowed them to remain submerged for up to a quarter of an hour before surfacing to breathe.

It was still daylight and the storm was subsiding as they crawled out on the rocky beach and clumsily heaved themselves above tideline. They were short-legged creatures with small strong forepaws. Their hind feet were webbed like a frog's and their long bodies were loosely wrapped in luxuriant fur coats, brown to near-black in color, with silver tips.

The otters were hungry but too tired to hunt for the crustaceans that clung thickly along the shoreward rocks. Those among them who could find space crawled into nooks and crevices. Some seemed to feel safer with just their heads thrust in among the rocks. A few stood erect for a while. Balancing on their hind feet, they gazed curiously about with their friendly, wide-apart eyes. The sound of the surf breaking upon the rocks lulled them. The land breeze carried no warning of danger. Soon all slept.

What happened, as the half moon rose above the shoreward cliffs, came from the water. Three long, narrow, skin-covered canoes, called *bidarkas*, came gliding soundlessly shoreward through the waves. In each craft were two men, the man in the stern plying a double-edged paddle, the one in the prow armed with a spear, clubs handy.

Light as cork the *bidarkas* were beached. Six Aleuts stepped out of the canoes, moving at once upon the sleeping band of sea otters. They were small, fur-clad men, their backs bent from long arching over paddles in their seal-skin craft. They moved as silently as stalking cats and killed swiftly with deft spear-thrusts. So experienced were they and adept with their weapons that many animals died without waking and their nearest companions slept on.

It was the cries of the otter pups being clubbed to death that roused the remaining animals. These lurched and scrambled toward the water, escaping into the surf.

Out of the band of a hundred sea otters some forty remained alive. The sixty-odd animals slaughtered on the rocky shore represented a great fortune in the fur trade at the turn of the century, when sea otter skins outranked even royal sable. But to the Aleuts who took all the risks, braving long voyages in their skin canoes, the reward was small. They had become virtual slaves of the European and Russian fur traders who were hunting the sea otter to the point of extinction.

For a time, out among the shoreward waves, sleek seal-like heads rose and sank, looking toward the beach. Some of their number might yet come out to them. While they waited, the Aleuts in the cove built a fire and began skinning out, also cooking some of the fresh meat, for they were hungry too.

The otters waited a long time but none joined them.

The remaining band did not go far that night, for shock and fatigue stopped them. On a kelp bed, a mile or so from shore, they set up a wailing lament for their lost mates and young. The females were loudest in their grief. They were devoted mothers and bore but a single pup a year. Sea otters are monogomous, taking one mate for life, so a lost mate meant a lonely life for the remaining partner.

The field of brownish seaweed, called kelp, swayed and rocked on the shoreward swells. It was buoyed by its hollow stems and pods, which acted as air sacs, and anchored by suction roots to the sea floor some five fathoms below. On this floating raft of weeds the otters were safe from their enemies of the sea. From the human enemy they were never safe, but surely he had taken his toll for this night. As the half moon sank, a few heads were still alert and watchful. One young female, whose mate was still beside her, pressed her head in among the kelp stems and lay still. Soon she would have a pup of her own.

In the morning the sea otters swam out to a larger kelp bed two miles farther from shore and began to dive for shellfish. The grieving mothers would not hunt or eat. Their lament still sounded and would continue for some days. There were more females than males, a few of them about to bear, though there was no special breeding or calving time for their breed. Sea otter young might be born at any season. Also, their wonderful coats remained prime the year round, making them vulnerable to the fur hunter in all seasons.

For survival they had been forced into the sea long ago. Generation by generation they had adapted to life in the water. Their hind feet grew larger, more webbed, their cylindrical tails flattened paddlewise, their jaws strengthened to crush shellfish and grind them with their broad, flat-crowned molars. For resting places there was the floating kelp mass. Such verdureless islands had become the sea otters' home.

On a day of low-hanging white mist so thick that sounds were muffled, the young she-otter came to her hour and Lutra was born (his name in the books was *Lutra canadensis*, signifying the otter species as a whole). For full nine months she had carried him and would nurse and closely guard him for six months more. He was almost as helpless as a human infant, but his eyes were wide open and he was fully furred in a soft coat of a somewhat lighter brown than his mother's. She tongued him thoroughly, turning him over and over. Then she clasped him to her breast with her forepaws and, floating on her back, let him nurse as mammals do.

When the sun went down Lutra's mother prepared them both for the night. Rolling over and over in a tangle of seaweed she wrapped the strands about them like a blanket. The strong rubbery stems not only kept them together but held them safely to their kelp island, which rocked and tossed in the night on broad, heavy swells sweeping shoreward from a distant storm at sea. There were always storms in these coastal waters but the otters loved the motion of the waves, and rough weather meant that no enemies could come close.

Lutra's mother was too happy having her pup in her arms to bother about eating for a day or two, but when hunger drove her to the sea floor for food, she carried her newborn cub with her. Instinctively Lutra held his breath. Holding him under one arm the she-otter dove with vigorous thrusts of her webbed hind feet. Down in the dim, wavery light she scrounged for a crab and was up again, still gripping her pup.

When he was a few days older his mother would sink from beneath Lutra, leaving him afloat on the surface while she hunted for food on the bottom. He was usually well fed and asleep on his back at the time. Sometimes he wakened to find himself alone, gently rocking on the swells. Floating was second nature and he wasn't afraid. He simply rocked and watched till his mother surfaced again.

But swimming had to be learned.

When his mother turned him face-down for his first swimming lesson Lutra was terrified and cried. Quickly she put him on his back again, the sea otter's favorite position. Soon she was taking him for longer rides out away from their kelp island, holding him on her stomach and sculling seaward with her broad tail. Lutra liked these rides very much but the moment she turned him face down in the water he was afraid again.

When she had been patient with him long enough the she-otter swam away from her cub and let him struggle. Lutra tried to follow her but could not control his movements, nor could he remember how to turn over and float on his back. He mewed and cried. His mother swam

round him splashing and gurgling to show him what fun it
was, but Lutra only threshed and whimpered. Finally she
took him in her arms again and let him nurse.

The next time out he did a little better. He could see
by the way his mother swooped and swirled that swimming
was truly a great thing, but though he had been born almost in the water he was still afraid of it. One day she kept
right on swimming away from him as if heading for the
open ocean. Lutra could not bear it. He churned his legs,
his flipper feet thrust back, and he was swimming! His
mother let him catch up with her and together they swam
back to the kelp field.

Diving was even harder than learning to swim. He
would plunge downward after his mother, only to pop up
again like a cork while she continued smoothly into the
depths. Returning to the surface with a clam catch, she
would crack and eat it while Lutra nursed. If she had
caught nothing she would lie breathing for a while, reoxi-
dizing her lungs, then go back to her hunting. Lutra had
got used to the crashing sounds his mother made before
eating. Usually she cracked the shell in her jaws. When it
was too hard for her she brought up a small flat stone and
beat her clam on it till the shell broke. With her pup pla-
cidly nursing, she spread the broken pieces on her chest
and proceeded to eat the soft flesh out of the shell.

There was a large male creature with splendid fur to
whom his mother seemed particularly attached. Lutra
made use of him by drying off on the big fellow's warm,
glossy coat and his father did not seem to mind. The three
of them were a happy family and often played together. His
mother would toss him in the air and catch him again like a
ball. Sometimes his sire joined them in this game. Or he
would swing Lutra by his arms till he chittered with enjoy-
ment. Other times, his mother would hide in a thicket of

kelp stems and he would hunt for her. When he couldn't find her he set up a cry and she reappeared with crooning sounds to comfort him. Later, when Lutra learned to hide, too, she would circle the spot as if he were too clever for her.

Play was also learning. Once Lutra heard a peculiar sound, a kind of beat in the sea which grew louder. He sensed fear in his mother and the feeling was conveyed to him so strongly that ever after that particular sound—the beat of the killer whale—meant gravest danger. When they heard it his mother would draw him high up on the kelp bed. Even this was not enough and she would burrow with him into the mass of stems. There they would stay till the sea gave no sound but its own rhythmic stirring.

Mostly play was fun for its own sake, ball games with a bladder of kelp, tag or snatch-and-run with a long stem of seaweed. The brown air bladders were buoyant and floated, dragged under water they popped right up again. His mother trailed a stem under his nose and then dove with it. Lutra wanted to chase her but he was still afraid to dive. When it was time for this lesson to be thoroughly learned she kept diving and leaving him alone on the surface waters.

At a distance, other members of the clan were frisking on the swells, so Lutra swam over there. Some of the older ones had fish dinners spread on their chests. One pup no larger than Lutra himself was playing with a bladder cluster. With a flick of the head he tossed it in the air, then caught it again in his jaws. His round, friendly eyes rolled toward Lutra inviting him to join in the game. Lutra seized the weed and spun away with it, the other pup right after him.

The chase led among the diners and the remains of a fiddler crab was jarred from the chest of an elder. There were no reproaches, the old one merely sank to retrieve his

half-eaten meal and Lutra rushed on. When the other pup
overtook him they tugged at opposite ends of the kelp stem
till it broke in half. Lutra dove with his piece and was
delighted to find that he could keep going down and down.
When the need for air brought him up he did not pop to the
surface as usual but swam up with an easy undulating motion like his mother's.

Lutra filled his lungs and tried another dive, but
popped right up. He breathed out and tried again: down,
down to the foggy green depths! It seemed that he had
discovered the secret for himself. Air in the lungs buoyed
one up just as it did a kelp bladder, but if you let the air out
before you dove you could stay down.

His mother had surfaced and was looking for him.
The next time she dove to the bottom Lutra went with her,
surprising her as well as himself.

Chimney in the Weed

While sunning themselves on a fine morning, several otter families were showing each other great affection. Mothers fondled their young, mates leaned together, their beautiful, loose coats shining in the sun. Pups frisked and rolled. Today there were sea birds standing around. Several plump burgomaster gulls courted each other at the water's edge. A pair of cormorants fished close by. One of the dark, long-necked birds had a catch bulging in the pouch under his bill but was looking for more.

Lutra and his friend gamboled among the stems to the very center of the kelp mass where they had discovered a bolt hole wide enough for an otter or two, with green water heaving beneath. It was kind of scary, but today they felt venturesome. Soon the two were gliding down the chimney of weed and plopping in the water. Down under the kelp island they swam through weed stems to the edge and dragged themselves out like a pair of tired voyagers. Lutra's family was the nearest group so both pups dried their sopping coats on warm parental fur.

Later Lutra tagged along when his mother hunted crabs on the bottom. The leggy, hairy creatures kept slithering away as if whisked by the wind. The she-otter reached into a crack where a crab had disappeared, thrusting in her whole arm, but her paw came out empty. They had to go up and breathe for a while. The next time down she was lucky and caught her squirming pincered prey by a leg. Lutra found an empty whelk shell and floated with the new toy balanced on his stomach while his mother ate her crab.

It was very satisfying for Lutra to have a friend who always seemed to be waiting for him at the edge of the weeds. Together the two did everything better and faster than either of them could do alone. They learned faster, too, always spurring each other on.

Down among the bottom rocks was a female octopus guarding her eggs. Alarmed, she would move speedily backward, shooting water out of a syphon just under her head. If they came too close to her cave she sucked back out of sight leaving a cloud of sepia ink outside her door. The otter pups tried to imitate the eight-armed mollusk's neat backward motion, tails curled up under, paws quivering, but to do it properly one needed to be boneless.

There was a school of cod that swam past the kelp bed, first one way, then the other, though a resident pair of barracuda took toll of them almost every time. The barracuda had prognathous jaws full of interlocking teeth which might have chopped through the bodies of young sea otters as well, but Lutra and his friend sensed the danger and kept their distance. Emulating barracudas, the two nipped each other's tails, which led to practicing evasive swirls, gyrations, convolutions and plain somersaults in the water —agility necessary for survival in the hungry sea.

Sometimes they caught things just for the fun of it—a limpet from the bottom rocks, a fingerling cod snatched from its school—but until they were weaned a pebble was just as interesting to them. The eating habits of his elders absorbed Lutra. Once his mother brought up two clams and cracked them together for a special treat. The moment she spread the food on her chest and began to eat, a big male swam close and snatched the ready meal for himself. He did not even bother to bear it away, simply turned over on his back and devoured it all, dribbling bits of shell from the sides of his mouth.

Some annoyance might have seemed natural, but Lutra's mother showed none. She simply fed her pup, then dove to hunt another clam.

Lutra noticed that several elders of the band seized their food in this way. It meant that others had to hunt longer and oftener to keep these individuals as well as themselves supplied, but none seemed to object. It was all in fun apparently. Lutra decided to try snatching food, too.

On a bright, cold morning a large male otter was floating on his back with a big crab spread out on his high, furry stomach. Lutra watched his chance, climbed up, seized the crab and slid back into the water. He swam fast expecting playful pursuit. There was none. Becoming curious he surfaced again, the crab still fast in his jaws. The large male lay floating as before. He seemed scarcely to have stirred but as Lutra swam nearer his head turned and he fixed him with a look. No more than that, yet Lutra dropped the crab, which sank and was lost. Then he too sank. When he needed air Lutra climbed out on the kelp and hid among the stems.

He stayed lost for a long time. Finally his friend came to find him and dug him out of the weeds. Together they waddled down to the brink, clumsy on their short legs, but once in the water they became suddenly graceful, undulating, angling, swooping. The two lanced down through sparkling surface waters into bands of blue-green, then deeper into pure dark blue and up again through turquoise into filtered gold like a pair of furry fish gone crazy. Breathe a while and dive again, the whole sea belonged to them!

They checked on the female octopus and found her outside her cave reaching with all eight arms into rock crannies in search of food. Swooping past, they startled her so that she inked up several yards of ocean. No cod today, and the barracuda were absent, but through curtains of waving green fronds mollusk eyes stared at them. Fish swam by, silver as glints of moonlight when they were below them, blue as sliding shadows when the two were looking down. Lutra found a nautilus he liked and his friend pried at a periwinkle stuck to a rock.

Somewhat inshore there was a shelf of submerged rock like a great table spread with living food, food with mouths feeding on other food. The two dislodged several mussels which clung there. They scared a crab sitting with spread pincers waiting for something to come near enough for him to grab. They watched a fish being swallowed by another fish.

They were tired and hungry now, ready to swim home and find their mothers, when a long dark shadow took shape out of the murk. It hung for a moment with its pale stare fixed upon them. A whip of the long sinuous body and the monster was alongside. Then a sidewise roll and it was under them, all white belly and gaping jaws showing a double row of saw-like teeth. The two young otters flung apart and streaked away. The shark tailed them closely, its long cylindrical body whipping toward one and then the other. After each belly-up glide and a chop that missed, the shark righted itself for forward motion, then rolled again to snap at their darting shapes.

Dodging, doubling spasmodically, the otters kept just beyond those jaws. They were running out of air and had to surface for a quick breath, then down again, for their speed was far greater submerged. The shark was faster but the slight pause it took to roll belly-up was the otters' one advantage.

The kelp bed loomed now, but with the shark so close upon them they dared not take time to clamber up. Lutra, with his friend following, kept going underneath the weed mass, through its trailing stems. The shark was slowed now, impeded by his own bulk in the twining weed. It was harder for him to roll and chop, hard even to see, but he was ravenous and would not give up. He hung there, watching for the prey to show through the tangle.

The otter pups pressed upward into the thickening weed. It became denser, but they had come down its chimney, there must be a way up. They had to find it soon, or drown, for their lungs were close to bursting from long submersion.

From above, the chimney had been a clear bolt hole, from below it was no more than a thinner place in the great kelp tangle. Suddenly, above showed a thin filter of light. They made for it and shot upward into the life-giving air.

On the swaying island above, a score or more of the otter clan lay basking and napping. Among them the otter pups found their anxious mothers, ready to fondle and feed them as if they were mere infants instead of the great adventurers they had become.

Beat of the Killer Whale

A year had passed. Lutra was largely on his own now, though his mother still watched over him and would continue to do so for two or three years more. Like human children, sea otter pups continue to learn over a long period. Their development is slower but more complete than most animals.

Lutra had discovered that the sea held many dangers as well as the food and the fun of life. What he had not yet learned was that for all its hazards the sea was safer for his kind than the land. Lutra had seen how his elders avoided the coasts and islands and he sensed their dread when boats passed or fires gleamed on far shores, but had not yet encountered the Great Enemy, man.

Elders had habits and privileges not shared by the young. Lutra had got used to this: the preempting of food by certain males cheerfully tolerated by the rest, the special preoccupation with each other at different times, often during storm when the kelp island rocked and rolled, these and other adult concerns largely excluded the young. But all played together, young and old, and when restlessness stirred in one, all seemed ready to go.

Certain seasons and weather so increased the band's venturesomeness that not even swimming out to meet and ride the tallest waves was enough. This was apt to come when land breezes laid a breath of mystery over the sea and faint scents came to them—sandy shores, rocky cliffsides, verdure. Once land as well as sea had belonged to them, and a different, lost life still faintly called to them from the shore. But there were elders among them whose memory of sudden lethal attacks by man constituted a protection to them all.

When land scents called and restlessness stirred in them, the band changed kelp islands. Suddenly a kind of current ran through them, soft calls and answers sounded in their midst and one and all plunged into the sea. They swam in close formation, face down, dipping under the waves. When it pleased them they stopped for hunting or play, or they might swim submerged for a while, always keeping close together and all filled with a fine sense of travel and change.

Sometimes they passed through a school of bass or cod moving seaward toward their spawning places. All around them the sea birds dipped and mewed as they snatched up fish, or rested upon the surface, too gorged to fly. Around the edges of the school dogfish snapped and darted, also sea pike and barracuda, all too sated from easy feeding to take any notice of the sea otter band passing by. They, too, fed on fish, surfacing to float and eat, enjoying their temporary immunity in the very midst of dangerous enemies.

Once, while Lutra and his parents and others were

breathing and eating at the outer edge of a migrating school, a black mountain suddenly rose from the sea. Thrusting upward slantwise, cataracts of water poured down its sides. Lutra was actually lifted by the mammoth shape and slid down its gleaming, black side. At the same instant a geyser shot into the air, spraying them all. In a leisurely way the mountain peak lowered and became a living, moving island.

Lutra was more awed than scared. No positive sense of fear came from his elders, though all veered quickly aside to be out of range of the sperm whale's flukes, which flung skyward for an instant, then struck the water with a crash that might have obliterated the whole clan. From the top of a swell Lutra watched as the black giant plowed once more into the school of cod. His vast jaws yawned open making a cavern that took in barrels of fish each time he snapped them closed. With a vigorous churning of feet and tail Lutra was treading water and standing high for a better view of this extraordinary giant eating his way through the school of fish and leaving a lane of clear water in his wake.

The sea otter band swam on, floating and frolicking in no hurry at all. The kelp island where they finally came to rest was much like the one they had left, but a submerged reef offered a change of fare, and for a time no restlessness moved them on.

The northern summer was at hand and flocks of birds were passing over from the south. The call was insistent, and suddenly all in a body the sea otters were on their way.

On this northern trip they were leisurely as always, stopping often for rest and sport. Lutra and his friend nosed into the fringes of weed that hung in many sea caves. They hunted the sandy bottoms shoreward for their favorite foods, and rode the heavy swells.

The third day a late spring storm plowed the surface of the sea and throbbed in the air. The more tumultuous the seas, the greater the sport. They frisked and dove and rode the smoking crests. Tired of play, the whole band sank to untroubled waters fathoms down.

They traveled mostly with the coastline in sight, all filled with a sense of destination, and there was great excitement in this. Land was a danger but land was a lure. It was exciting just to touch ground in the growing season, brief as it was in the north.

After the storm had passed, a light mist lay over the waters and there was softness in the air. More than ever now the elders of the band seemed to know what they were about, and led the way with assurance. They were in a kind of pass between small islands. Lutra kept pushing ahead, impatient to crawl out upon some new shore.

Abruptly nervousness pervaded the swimming band. The new feeling overrode all eagerness and anticipation. Lutra sensed it even before he heard the *beat* in the sea, the same sound which used to make his mother hide him in the kelp when he was small. Once when he had popped out of the hole she had just pressed him into, Lutra had seen a row of black fins cutting the water near their island. Shuddering with fear, his mother had thrust him down again into the weeds.

Her danger signal was sounding now and Lutra heard the same from others of the band. The signal meant *swim as fast as you can.*

The sound grew. It was an up and down pulse that came through the waters, a steady rhythmic beat that told of large, heavy bodies rushing toward them. The otters could swim no faster than they were going, their fear was paralyzing, slowing them down.

Fear of the *orca*, or killer whale, was as ingrained as the fear of man and almost as great. The killer whale was the sea otters' enemy of enemies of the sea, as man was of the land. Both were kill-crazy, and neither knew any limit to his greed.

The band had turned toward the nearest of the small islands. Those in the lead might make it in time, but many would not, for by this time the killers were close and there was a whole pack of them swimming abreast, some leaping clear of the water in sheer blood lust. Killers were always ravenously hungry and it took vast amounts of food to satisfy their thirty-foot bodies, each weighing some eight thousand pounds.

Lutra's mother was signaling him again. She and others about him were acting in a way that seemed senseless to the fleeing pup: suddenly they were lying very still, like old, dark pieces of wood drifting toward shore. The sharp chittering sound she made indicated that he was to do the same. The *orcas* were almost upon them, there was no possibility of outdistancing them to the shore. All around him members of their band had turned to short logs drifting on the current. Lutra, too, became driftwood.

The great bodies threshed about nearby and jaws chopped. Lutra heard death cries from his own kind, but he neither moved nor blinked an eye and soon the killers rushed on in search of larger fare.

Abruptly, the driftwood otters came to life. Lutra in their midst was swept into the shallows and finally ashore. His mother kept going higher and higher among the rocks, still hustling him along. Above the tideline she hid herself in a cranny. Lutra too found a hole to crawl into and lay hidden for a long time.

The Seal Islet

For days after their terrifying experience with the killer whales the otter band nursed its grief. The wailing of the lonely ones filled the air. Lutra, too, was lonely. He kept calling and searching for his friend. Perhaps his friend might come out of some secret place where he had been hiding, or be waiting for him at the tide's edge when he slid into the water. But his friend never came.

The small island was inhabited only by birds. It was a place where ships never came and man had left few if any traces, but the elders were watchful. And all knew instinctively that at any moment the enemy might come. At night two or three stood guard, erect as posts, listening tensely for the slap-and-drip of paddles approaching the shore.

But nights passed like the days—peacefully. The band, what was left of it, reveled in the tingling summer softness, warmth underlaid with coolness, balmy days now twenty hours long. Land. It satisfied that deeper need which had drawn them north. Also, the islet provided them with rich and varied feeding.

Tender grass grew in the tidal pools and a species of sand crab scuttled there, scarcely more than a morsel to eat but fun to scramble after. There were sea urchins and other shellfish on the sandy bottoms. Mussels clung to the rocks, lively crabs lived in crannies eroded by the waves. Yet not even the younger otters allowed themselves to overeat. Life itself might depend on fitness and speed.

Waking one morning, Lutra was surprised to see a crowd of long, sleek strangers stretched out on the rocks at the water's edge. All were much larger than his own kind and some were really monstrous with heavy bodies and bristling whiskers. These were so startling that Lutra went back into the rock crevice where he had slept and just watched.

None of the visitors had legs. Moving, they heaved themselves about or waddled on broad flat flippers. In the water they shot through waves, looped and dove in shiny dark arcs to the bottom and up again. While Lutra watched, several of them surfaced with live, flapping fish in their mouths. One playfully tossed a fish to a neighbor who caught and swallowed it, all in a single movement. They were quite noisy, barking and coughing in and out of the water, but all seemed to be enjoying themselves. From time to time the mammoth ones lifted their heads from their heavy wrinkled necks and bellowed.

Now Lutra noticed that several members of his own clan were going about their affairs in the very midst of these strangers. He saw one of the otter elders pass between a pair of them, almost brushing against their sleek sides.

Presently his own mother came out of the water with a catch and two or three of the visitors watched with mild interest while she knocked her clam on a rock to break the shell.

Evidently these strangers meant them no harm. Lutra moved out of his cranny and joined his mother, who gave him a bite of her clam. Later, in the water, large, dark shapes coated with silvery bubbles swam past him, but there was no sense of threat or danger. They were swooping after fish and catching them too! Lutra would have liked to join them in their fun, but he wasn't fast enough.

The seals chose to remain and the two clans lived together harmoniously. Actually, they helped each other, for the seals' big bodies plunging through the offshore depths stirred up all manner of otter fare, and the female seals enjoyed the company of the mother otters in their favorite sunning places. Some of these appeared to look on the smaller otters as their own young and would roll close to them with soft urking cries. The seals were increasingly vocal and enthusiastic about everything, which might have proved disturbing, but the otters adjusted to the noise.

Abruptly one day the cow seals ceased shooting through the depths to hunt and play and began to give birth to the calves of that season. One or two convulsive heaves, and there was an almost white baby seal lying beside its mother, the short umbilical cord breaking as she turned over. Afterwards the cow seal went into the water to wash herself and then she fed the baby.

Lutra took wondering note of the increasing numbers. Sea-bird families on the higher rocks also had young, and the parent birds skimmed the surface waters diving for small fish that they might feed to their fledglings. The cries of these added to the seals' clamor. It was a busy noisy colony of creatures, all smelling of fish.

Baby seals had to learn to swim just like young otters. They liked the water and would lie in the shallows letting the waves wash over them, but panicked if a receding wave drew them into deep water. Sometimes the mother seal supported her infant by slipping beneath him, but soon she was letting him founder till his own flippers came into action. Baby seals quickly learned to swim, but diving lessons took a bit longer. As with the otter pups they had to learn to expel their breath in order to stay down.

Soon the young seals were swimming and diving with the rest of them. They were pleasant playmates for Lutra, who took long swims with them every day. Almost before he knew it, the baby seals were bigger than he was and already they were masters of their element. In games of tag Lutra was usually left behind. When they bumped into him accidentally, he bounced.

One of the weaker baby seals, who didn't grow as fast as the others, became Lutra's special friend. When Lutra dove, leading the way among the sea caves and grottos hung with weeds, his seal friend followed devotedly. When the young seal chose to lead, Lutra followed willingly and tried to catch a fish. The two skimmed along the sandy sea floors watching for faint stirrings that told of plaice or flatfish in hiding, tender special feeding that both liked.

Once, adventuring with the seal pup, Lutra saw a pale tentacle just disappearing into an underwater cave. Gaily he went after it, intent on showing his friend how octopi suck backward in fright when swimmers approach their grottos. But this octopus did not behave like the female with the eggs that he remembered having fun with when he was young. For one thing, this octopus was larger.

Barely within the narrow cave entrance, the friends stopped at what they saw: a stirring of coil upon coil of pallid tentacles, and in the vast, pale body an eye that fixed and held them horror struck. The seal was gone in a flash. Lutra back-flipped and shot toward the opening, but a tentacle of the octopus already had him. It was a half-loop about his middle, and Lutra felt the suction tip striving for a hold on his back. The thick fur there was a poor surface for a grip. Lutra's heavy pelt and his strong jaws, which were capable of cracking clam shells, saved the day for him. He chopped frenziedly at the pale loop which held him, finally severing the tip. Out into the deep blue he shot before a second tentacle could reach him, then up through the blue-green to the surface.

He had brought with him the severed tentacle tip and now, floating on his back, he proceeded to eat it while his seal friend watched.

The fur seals' mating time had come, and pandemonium broke loose. The sea colony became positively tumultuous with sound. All day, the bull seals roared challenges, each herding as many cows as possible into his own chosen section of rocky shore. There were swift short battles between them, none lethal, but accompanied by fierce coughing bellows, the cows setting up a clamor of their own.

After a day or two of this the peace-loving otter clan could stand no more. They left in a body for the nearest weed mass, and the life of the kelp beds was resumed. Lutra missed his seal friend, and all missed the rich, easy feeding around the islet. Here there were no mussels clinging to the rocks, no small crabs skittering in and out of crannies. Clams were scarce, too—harder work for smaller fare. But there was peace and quiet. The landward breeze brought them far sounds of the seal colony, and the otters listened as they rocked and swayed on the tidal roll.

The nights were growing longer and colder. Great shoals of fish began moving past the otters' island to their spawning places in the southwest. Birds wheeled restlessly above them, preparing for the flight south. The first of the fall storms brought stinging rain out of the northeast with winds that moaned high above. The sea birds were swept from the sky and gathered in great rafts to ride out the gale. It was hard on the gulls and kittiwakes, but the sea otters were exhilarated. The more their kelp bed rocked and heaved, the better, and they went out to meet the tallest waves. All welcomed the sense of change that was in the air.

When the storm had blown itself out there was warmth and calm again, almost like spring. All weather was good, but the evanescent warmth teased them into wanting the land again. As if by common consent they left the kelp bed and headed back to the rocky islet. They would be glad to see their seal friends and gladder still to feed up on crabs and mussels before the cold drove them southward.

Halfway to the islet a sense of uneasiness slowed the elders, and the rest of them automatically waited. Presently they heard the seals, but something was wrong. The band swam slowly now, some of them treading water the better to peer, noses high winnowing the breeze. A few even shaded their eyes with a paw, as a man might do in sunlight.

A sudden signal from the leader meant *full stop, go no further.* When a shoreward swell lifted him, Lutra saw two boats beached on the rocky shore and four men moving around. The elders were chattering with terror, warning them of gravest danger so that dread filled them all. Lutra felt it, too, though he had never seen human beings before.

On the shore the men were making a great noise to drive the seals up among the rocks away from the water.

The hard slapping reports of rifle fire came ricocheting across the water. The otter clan could not see all the brutal action that followed, but blood memory brought them the horror of it all. The shots they heard were killing the mature seals, the smaller ones were being clubbed to death, as was the custom of fur hunters.

The slaughter went on. Cries of the dying reached them over the water. A few of their former friends escaped into the sea, but none of the calves. Whimpering, the otter band rounded and swam back to the kelp island.

The Caught One

A cold wind was howling down from the Bering Sea, plow-ing the waters to great depths, pressing gray-black cloud masses down to meet the waves. The kelp island heaved and rolled. Loose stems threshed and writhed as if they would unwind the compact mass and float it away.

Lutra had buried himself deep in the weeds but he was uncovered and all but flung from his hole. He was not alarmed, nor was he surprised to see many of the mature members of the band happily coupled in the weeds. Stormy weather was stimulating to them; also there was a sense of security in being shut in by the storm.

Storm zeal filled Lutra. He stood erect among the whipping stems, facing into the gale. He was past two now, large for his age, though not yet mature. His sleek head was a series of rounds: round low brow, small round ears, round brown eyes in a friendly, whiskery face. His rich, brown fur was underlaid with a downy undercoat of a paler color. He was four feet long, including his broad, tapering tail, with muscles hard as cables. Though at one with his clan, he was beginning to feel independent in a way that put new demands upon him. He had much to prove to himself, and the will to do it.

Cloud and water were one driving mass, a delirious excitement which somehow had to be acted upon. Lutra skittered between the loving couples to the edge of the kelp field, lanced into a heaving sea and dove through the roiled waters to the relatively calm depths. Some of the foam bubbles and wildness seemed to have got into his blood. He joined a passing school of mackerel, thousands strong, wove and cork-screwed through their midst so that they darted in alarm, and swam with them at their own speed. In the silvery, slithery press of fish he felt a need for air and right-angled, then whipped his body like a water snake and shot upward. At the periphery of the school he caught two small fish. With one of these in his jaws and the other under his arm, he surfaced and swam for home.

Before it subsided the wind brought sheets of almost liquid ice which flattened and darkened the sea. Soon winter would close in and the northern waters would be barren of much of the ottters' fare. The band began to drift south.

It was not a migration, simply a movement in tune with what was going on in sea and sky. Pollock hordes moved beneath them, going south and west. Above in high sky the late stayers, geese and cranes, passed southward in stately Vs. Occasionally tattered wedges of water fowl shot past like bullets. Out of the Aleutians, those seven hundred tiny islands that were the breeding place of storms, bad weather spawned unceasingly. The otters rode the waves or wended the quiet deeps, rising as necessary to reoxidize their lungs.

There were rocky reefs where they rested and fed and

sometimes met danger. Once, a pair of blue sharks waited for them in an islet among the rocks of a weed-grown reef. As the twenty-foot monsters came gliding out of the weed-hung murk the otters scattered in panic. The blues gave only short chase, then headed seaward as if answering a call. The otters were tired but they shunned that reef, continuing southward by mutual consent. Later they passed up a small island, for upon them still was the memory of the slaughter of their seal friends. What the band finally settled for was another kelp bed, the one trusted refuge.

On a rare quiet day when the band rested, Lutra heard cries coming through the mist. He had been foraging on the bottoms and had the remains of a crab spread on his chest. He chewed, listened, chewed again. From time to time it sounded like several cries, all identifiably otter, and seemed to come from different directions. Perhaps another otter clan was nearby and would presently join them, as sometimes happened when their numbers were depleted by fur hunters.

There were nearer sounds, the voices of his own band feeding and frisking about. Lutra lost track of that other voice, and then it came again more clearly. It was a call, and its sender was frightened and alone. Lutra was curious. The mist made all sounds confusing but he tried first one direction, then another, the diffused cries drawing him nearer shore.

What he heard now was a pitiful wail, followed by a furious, chattering complaint. The terror in the sounds pierced him, the fear in them was his own. But he had to go and see.

The cries came from a narrow reef with a jagged spine of rock. Lutra swam to it and found one of his own kind, a small female with a white head, lying on the tide-washed shelf. She seemed mysteriously caught there and chirred at him fiercely, as if he were to blame for it all. Then she gave another long wail of pain. Close to her as he was, Lutra could only wail too. The shock of this stopped her at once.

When he nudged her to get her on her feet she bit him wildly. The sudden hurt might have driven him away, but the next instant she was attacking a trap that held her. It was a spring trap with a chain fastened to a rock, and the she-otter was caught by a hind leg. Lutra bit the trap, too, trying to help. His powerful jaws closed on the metal and his teeth scored it, but the steel band held. He tried again, and must have jerked at it, for in a frenzy of pain she bit at herself and at him. Lutra subdued her with a threatening *aur-gh!* and continued to bite and leap upon the trap. This female was a demented creature, dangerous to herself and to him, but he couldn't leave her the way she was. He had to fight the thing that held her fast.

After a time the caught one sagged strangely, going limp as a dead thing. Lutra redoubled his attack on the trap, lifting and shaking the thing, flinging his full weight upon it and thumping it with his powerful hind feet. No knowing which of his galvanic efforts pressed down the clamp and released the steel jaws, but suddenly it happened, the cruel teeth fell apart.

The young female was caught no longer, but she was still limp. Lutra went on battling the trap. His jaws were bleeding and he was exhausted before he saw that she had roused and was quietly gazing at him, her freed leg drawn up under. Lutra dropped where he was and slept.

Her sharp chittering roused him. She was standing beside him, very agitated. Through the mist came a strange un-animal-like sound, the faint rub and creak of oarlocks. To Lutra it meant little, but her terror was warning

enough. Together they dove, and Lutra shot away. She was
slower. It was now in the water that her hurt appeared, the
leg that had been caught in the trap lacked the necessary
thrust. He slowed for her and she followed close as his own
tail back to the kelp field where his band was at rest.

The elders were aware of the boat that had come out to
the reef. This particular kelp bed was too close to shore for
safety. The band pushed off, resuming the intermittent passage down the coast. The young female was one of them
now, as if she had always belonged, and Lutra's mother
included her in the special watchfulness still reserved for
her son. Their speed was automatically slowed to her pace,
for always the band moved as one creature.

Moving out to sea, they encountered a smaller band
of otters also moving south, probably the company to
which the young female had belonged. These sought to join
the larger group and were accepted. Lutra's band was now
restored to its former size of some sixty-odd, large for these
grim times, though once the sea otter herds had numbered
many hundreds of animals.

Imatuk, the caught one, healed well and regained her
former agility, but the pain and terror of her encounter
with man left their mark on her spirit. She had memory
moods that made her shrewish. She would wind herself in
weeds and chitter fiercely at any who came near, with the
exception of Lutra. Him she tolerated at all times, as if
never quite forgetting that he was her rescuer and had
saved her life.

In happier moments Imatuk was a good playfellow.
She and Lutra chased and frolicked. They played ball with
air bladders and had tugs of war with the stems. They
basked entwined. Sometimes Lutra centered her on a rock
or weed clump and frisked about her, going through his

whole gamut of acrobatics till she blinked and closed her eyes several times. He would spiral-dive to the bottom, she following. In ordinary foraging among the submerged rocks Imatuk was better than he, quicker to see the disappearing claw or the stir of sand that meant a flatfish in hiding. She was very neat about her person, endlessly combing and grooming her beautiful coat. Sometimes she basked in the sun beside Lutra's mother, for they were close companions. Imatuk was always there, eating and sleeping as close to Lutra as possible. But they were merely playfellows. Maturity for them both was still a long way off.

The band moved in its leisurely fashion. They had evaded the intense cold of the Aleutians and the Bering Sea. Now, off the Canadian coast, there was the slow moving Kuroshio current coming northward from Japan. It was warm enough to keep the seas from freezing, and shellfish abounded. Loitering now, they were joined by the survivors of three other small bands, sad creatures still grieving over the loss of mates or offspring. For the older ones there were shuddery warnings in these depleted companies.

The remnant clans that had joined them numbered less than a single band a few seasons before, and their nervous fears were catching. Imatuk especially sensed their sorrow. She brooded and wouldn't play. Lutra gamboled and clowned to beguile her, but she ignored him, hiding her head among the weeds.

The leaders were more wary now. They chose kelp beds farther and farther from the coast. But poor feeding forced them inland, so it was the reefs again. On one of these which was almost awash at high tide, sole and flatfish hid in thick beds on the sandy bottoms. A large barracuda hid also, watching for larger fish or anything he could snatch, including unwary sea otters. He was a loner and an

old one, more dangerous than a shark, for with his croco-
dile jaws he could attack head on and fast, without the
need to turn belly-up.

Lutra made a game of keeping tabs on this menace,
and kept Imatuk wary of his lurking presence, but others of
the band were less sharp. Two were caught and devoured.
This made the barracuda even more voracious. The band
was forced to leave his chosen range for another reef farther down the coast.

This roomy ridge of rock seemed a perfect place to
stay awhile, except that Imatuk's repeated cries of warning
kept them all on edge. Some faint intimation of man had
reached her through the air or the water and she was not
about to forget it. To the rest of them there was no sign or
scent of danger. The visible shoreline seemed uninhabited,
no fires glowed there in the night, no boats passed by. The
band remained.

Failing to rouse the older ones Imatuk concentrated
on Lutra. Her complaints filled his ears. She would not
play, and soon she was refusing to eat as well. It was flight
she was urging, but that was impossible unless all went
together. Lutra wearied of her nagging and set off for some
fun all by himself. Imatuk tagged along but he could out-
swim her anytime. When he surfaced for air he saw her
white head small with distance.

While he hunted below she caught up and waited for
him to eat his catch, but she wouldn't be quiet. Some of the
sounds she made were like those she had made in the trap.
In a dark, instinctive way Lutra was touched. He had to
hearken. He had to heed.

Some nights later, under a full moon, a boat with
three men came out of a hidden inlet and started for the
reef. Instantly, Imatuk had uprisen and was giving the

alarm. She had sounded off too many times before and might have been ignored, but Lutra joined her, adding his warning call for all to hear. Out of the clefts and crannies where they had hidden themselves for sleep, the band assembled. After listening intently for a time they moved in a body to the water's edge and dove.

When the fur-hunters arrived with their guns and clubs they found nothing but bare moonlit rocks.

Imatuk

Two springs later, the sea otter band was up near the Aleutians again, where their diminishing kind was drawn more and more for what safety might be left to them. They were living on a large, high-riding field of kelp, its surface a forest of thick fronds which gave them a sense of privacy and refuge. Their occasional urge to hide could be totally satisfied in these dense weeds. Even Imatuk seemed almost happy here and unusually good-tempered.

Lutra had come into full maturity. He was some five feet long now, weighing close to seventy-five pounds, and his coat had the luster of all rare things. It seemed to glow from within with glints of gold in its brown. A frosting of silver at the tips made him seem larger than he was, though he was maximum size for his kind, with strength and sagacity equalled by few.

Imatuk too was coming into her prime, sleek and glowing, though still rather small. Her dark, shining eyes in the pale, soft fur of her face had a special appeal and the smooth, rippling grace of the sea was in all her movements. To keep close track of Lutra seemed her main concern in life. Day and night she was at his side and growing ever more affectionate. She was also more willing to play or hunt or bask, all as Lutra might choose.

The northern summer days were almost endless and the land breeze brought them the scent of growing, blooming plants, but the otter band was too wise to be drawn ashore. Not but what the enemy hunted them at sea as well. They had experienced several surprise attacks in the past two years, and had escaped many more.

There was no safe place for their kind these days, and all vaguely sensed this. But far more vivid to them were the joys of life in the sea and on the kelp floes with each other. Their whiskers twitched with the pleasure of tweaking a friend's tail, or cutting past a swimmer's nose to start an underwater chase. And one taste of clam or crab or sea urchin was worth hours of scrounging on the bottoms. If a hungry elder came and took one's catch, that was fine too.

Lutra lay rocking on the swells with a long section of seaweed in his jaws. Imatuk was supposed to come and snatch it, but she was pretending not to see him at all. Shading her eyes with a paw she gazed seaward, then dove neatly, tail over head, and came up behind him. Without turning, Lutra bit off a length of weed and tossed it in the air. He caught it again as it came down and gave the thing a good shaking. This was too much. Imatuk lanced in, snatched the kelp stem he was chewing on and made off with it seaward. Lutra gave chase and there was a big scramble. At the end of this game there was nothing left of the kelp stem but one rubbery leaf and an air bladder, and it was in Imatuk's jaws.

She carried it back to the kelp bed and the two flopped down to rest in the horizontal evening sunlight. Presently Imatuk's white head was on Lutra's chest, her paws drawn up to cover her eyes as for sleep. Great good feelings were upon Lutra. Suddenly all the vague urgencies of his being came to a focus in the need for a mate and, wonderfully, the mate was at hand.

There was no going apart for nuptials. All around them the clan moved about the usual affairs of hunting, feeding, swimming, resting, and things went on happening. A baby otter was born back among the kelp stems and there was tragedy in the water near at hand. A year-old pup was caught by a dogfish. His mother rushed to the rescue and herself became the victim of a cruising shark attracted to the scene by blood in the water.

None took particular notice of the new mates, save perhaps Lutra's mother, yet all somehow radiated approval of the union. For Lutra there was bewilderment in this great new attachment to one who had frequently been something of a pest. But Imatuk took all their joys for granted, as if she had known from the beginning that they were destined to be mates.

Hunting together had new drama and charm. The feeding was good, the season was at its height, all things conspiring for their continued pleasure. And the vicissitudes of life in the sea kept their excitement at high pitch.

At any time at all out of the ragged mist or the rolling tides there might appear a line of tall black fins that meant killer whales. For the beat of these one always listened, and scurried to safety at the first faint sound. But there were other monsters as formidable in bulk that were harmless to frisk among. Blackfish, a northern species of the whale tribe, were huge and blunt-headed, yet mild-eyed and jolly looking as they floated and spouted on the surface.

Blackfish liked to rub against rocks to curry their thick hides, and it was the kind of sport that Lutra and Imatuk went in for these days to dart between the itching monster and his scratching rock. Naturally this took perfect timing. There was further risk in the lash of the blackfish flukes. The object of this game was to be lifted and flung skyward on the wave created by the slap of the great horizontal tail. To be in the right spot at the exact right moment for this took all their dexterity, as well as their speed.

The two learned by experience that the swordfish, though armed and deadly, had to charge in a straight line. They could outmaneuver him anyday. They could also outmaneuver most sharks. Such hereditary enemies provided a fine workout for taut muscles and flexible bones.

The days of summer enchantment were coming to an end, not only for Lutra and his mate, but for the band as well. There was a sense of seasonal change and uncertainty. All were becoming restless again and there was nowhere to go, no kelp floes equal to the one they were on, only small patches floating about. When they moved from here it must be a fairly long carry southward.

As always the coastal shores called, but the enemy was there. If the older members of the band were unaware of human activities on the distant shore, Imatuk was not. She was in a state of nerves again and mewed and chittered, standing tall among the fronds, or hiding herself for long hours. Now her warnings were respected for she had been right more than once and had saved them all from grave harm. But she had also been wrong more than once, merely causing uneasiness and bother. This seemed one of those times, for there was no human scent on the breeze.

Lutra brought Imatuk a present of two smooth stones from the sea floor. She ignored his gift. He tried dragging a length of kelp past her foot and then diving with it. She made no move to follow. After a while he came back and affectionately dried his sopping coat on her soft fur. Imatuk allowed this but would not hunt with him, not even when he discovered a colony of cuttlefish in a cave among the bottom rocks.

After a time, Lutra gave up trying to lure her out and sought whoever would play with him. Two younger males were more than willing to chase and tag him and be tagged in their turn. Hungry after their sport, Lutra and his friends brought up a small cuttlefish, each of them gripping a tentacle. Not even this delicacy drew Imatuk out of her dark mood. Her gaze was fixed landward. Her round white head kept turning and lifting to scan the coastline. There was nothing unusual so far as Lutra could see, but he sat down close beside her.

The Kills in the Kelp

A northeast breeze was raising choppy waves that morning and it seemed to be herding several small rafts of weed toward the sea otters' island. These were the floating kind of seaweed with roots in the air, with which the north coastal waters abounded. Now and again one of the otter clan would raise up and stand at full height gazing landward. One elder shaded his eyes with a paw and stared for a long moment. Evidently satisfied that there was nothing suspicious about the approaching spread of weeds, he turned away.

Imatuk had been watching at the shoreward edge of the floe since first light. Occasionally, very agitated, she spun round uttering nervous cries, then she stiffened to attention as before. Lutra watched with her until hunger drove him to the hunt. Soon he was back again, staring

with her across the water, roused in spite of himself by his
mate's unwavering concentration. Some of the floating kelp
clumps were nearer than before, but that was not unnatural
with an offshore breeze.

Abruptly Lutra was watching as intently as Imatuk
herself. Two of the weed clumps were sliding forward, not
just an aimless turning with the waves, but directed movement toward their island. Imatuk set up a shrill chattering,
forepaws tight to her breast. Somehow, unknowably, the
enemy was near.

On a lift of breeze the human scent reached them.
With a cry of terror Imatuk disappeared through a hole in
the kelp. Lutra shrilled forth warnings, startling the band to
full attention as he flung himself through the ranks toward
the opposite side of the field. By this time two of the mys-
terously directed kelp clumps had heaved upward, reveal-
ing canoes, and now crashing reports echoed across the
water. Several of the clan dropped and lay twitching among
the kelp stems.

There was a sudden burn of pain across Lutra's neck
where a bullet had seared. The shock of it spun him round
and down in a sick flounder, but an instant later he was
crawling toward the water. In the green depths beneath the
weed floe the remaining ones, including Imatuk—but not
Lutra's mother—rallied about him, and the band, such as it
was, sped seaward together.

In the season which followed, the sea otter clan
moved many times in search of kelp floes isolated enough
to offer them sanctuary. Toward spring, they were joined
by two other decimated bands. Increased numbers helped
to restore their confidence. If only they could find a home,
a safe place for them all to settle down.

On a remote floe out of sight of land Imatuk's pup

was born, a fine little male with a head as round and white as her own. The most rapt and attentive of mothers, Imatuk guarded her young one with fanatical zeal. When she wasn't floating with the pup in her arms, feeding and comforting him, she was tonguing his soft fuzzy coat, cleansing him from head to foot.

Lutra was allowed to bask beside them in times of rest. He watched tolerantly while Imatuk tossed their offspring in the air and caught him again, squeaking with pleasure. At sunset, when she rolled herself and her infant into a wrapping of kelp stems, he stood guard.

Watching over his family, Lutra would feel a sudden urge toward the edge of the kelp field where he would stand testing the water sounds, sifting the landward breeze. He had acquired the habit of caution from his overanxious mate, but he had learned from experience that not even the kelp floe, where no other creature could survive, was safe from the two-legged enemy with sudden death in his hands.

Lutra had not forgotten those terrifying blasts of sound, or the writhing ones among the kelp stems, or his own searing pain. It meant that he could never become quite heedless again, or trust to others the responsibility for his clan's safety.

Among the dying ones on the day when the weed rafts hid the enemy had been several leaders of the band. Lutra had not sensed that he was acting as they would have done when he hustled the remaining ones to the comparative safety of the sea. It was still not clear to Lutra that the band looked to him for guidance, even as he looked to Imatuk to warn of imminent danger.

Soon the white-headed pup was being taught to swim. Imatuk would not leave him floating in the usual way during her absences on the sea floor, so Lutra went along for the swimming lessons. It began to appear that Imatuk was afraid to turn the pup face downward in the sea, as must be done if he was ever to master the element, so it was Lutra who performed this duty also. The pup learned quickly enough, imitating the motions of his sire.

When it came to the diving lesson, Lutra expelled his own breath close to the pup's ear and dove. After repeating the process several times, the pup caught on and blew in Lutra's ear. A few failures, then he was breathing out and staying down. Soon the white-headed pup was doing tail-over-head dives and seal-like loops, boring through the waves like a small porpoise.

Mostly he was supposed to stay with his mother, but once, on the way to the bottom, Lutra found his son close-tailing him in deep water, and tailing the pup in the blue dimness was the long dark shape of a hunting mackerel shark. Looping upward, Lutra caught the pup under one arm and was away at a flashing tangent.

The sudden change in the size of his prey evidently confused the mackerel shark, for he veered from side to side in hesitation, then abruptly abandoned the chase.

In a spring storm the sea otters' isolated kelp island broke its root moorings and blew toward shore. The ride on the pitching, turning weed delighted them all. When the heavy seas massed the fronds, they played hide-and-seek among the humps and knots of weed. Part of the time they were in the water or swimming underneath their former home, then up again riding, not to miss a thing.

When the kelp mass approached the shore the band pitched off and swam to a rocky reef for the night. With the first light they were off again, not even trusting the mist and flying scud to hide them from possible enemies.

Hordes of fish were moving northward. In their wake came the gluttons, the gorgers—sharks, barracuda, sea pike; all very dangerous to young pups. Lutra and Imatuk kept close watch over their offspring, both in and out of the water. The band had found a massive kelp bed out of sight of land. In the thick forest of weed the white-headed pup could sleep in safety, or play games with others his age. He could dive through bolt holes in the bare, rubbery stems and come to more delicate stems growing up like bushes from the sea floor, some of them tender and good to eat. He could, but what he liked was to go with his sire.

Perhaps because he had had a large part in the play-teaching of his offspring, Lutra had a hero-worshipping pup to worry about. Wherever he went to hunt or explore, even into the caves and grottos of octopi, the white-headed one was likely to tail him. Eager and trustful, he was necessarily Lutra's first concern, thus curtailing his old freedom. The pup was already a fine and agile swimmer. To stay with Lutra in the depths he had early learned the need for quick reoxidation of his lungs. A few breaths on the surface, and tail-over-head he was back in the depths, a worry and distraction to his sire.

What the pup had not learned, with two attentive parents to watch over him, was the lesson of survival in the sea—the need to be afraid. Not even a brush with a hunting shark taught him that lesson. Lutra bore all the strain of the encounter. Acting in the only way to save his own and the young one's life, Lutra swam under the shark when he bellied up to snap at them, and over the shark when he righted himself for forward movement. At his side or tail in each maneuver, the precocious pup enjoyed the new game and was good at it. When they gained the kelp bed unhurt the pup wanted to play the game again.

The white-headed pup had to learn fear for himself. On the bottom, some seventy feet down, Lutra was busy loosening some mussels from the rocks. The pup had been with him but was suddenly gone. Nearby was the dark mouth of a cave. Lutra shot through the opening into the deep grotto beyond. In the dimness pale tentacles showed, also the white head of his son.

With an octopus the one hope was to act quickly before too many tentacles came into play. The pup was paralyzed with fright but as his sire's powerful jaws went to work on the crushing loop that held him, he, too, bit and snapped at it. The mollusk was not as big as the one Lutra had tangled with in his younger days, but this octopus was ravenous, and they were trespassers on its preserve.

For the otter pair the greatest danger was the ever-present need for air. The pup was strong-lunged for his age, but shock and fear had exhausted him, and he was weakening. Lutra's shell-grinding jaws must work fast. Just as he severed the tentacle that held his offspring another whipped out to replace it and a third was striving to wrap itself around Lutra's head.

The combined clutch might have held them there until the pup, at least, had drowned, but instinct drove Lutra in for a jaw-hold on the pulpy head. Even so, it was moments before pain and panic made the octopus loosen all holds and shoot backward.

Making for the surface, Lutra had a limp pup under his arm, but he revived quickly, and for once was as glad to see his mother as she was to see him. Glad even to stay with his mother for a while, letting his sire hunt alone and in peace.

Birds were streaming up the coast, low over the water on calm clear days, high in stormy weather. Their travel cries coming down the wind filled the otter clan with an Aleutian urge, but all along the way the human enemy was rife. Imatuk was all nerves again, watching the shoreward waters in her spooky way, concentrating on a distant reef. Sometimes she whimpered like a creature in pain. Was it coming disaster that she sensed, or nothing at all?

Lutra watched for a tangible sign, but the days passed and there were no night flares to landward, no creeping kelp patches or scent of man on the wind. But there was uneasiness of spirit. He too felt that. He began moving through the band, intimating in slight but telling ways that it was time to go. Gradually all were roused, and on a gray, windless morning the little company of tag-end bands set off together.

Imatuk's nervousness had taken a new turn. Distrusting the kelp floes that were the last recourse of their kind, she circled every weed-bed before climbing out for rest. When the band was tired and hungry an extra trip round their chosen resting place, with delays for sniffing and air-testing, was not to be borne. From long experience Lutra let her be his guide, and there were those who followed him in all that he did, but the newer members of the band disregarded Imatuk's promptings and clambered upon any weed mass that was handy.

At the end of a long, windy day off the Alaskan coast they reached a kelp island familiar to them from years past. To suspect this old home was too much. Lutra himself was at the point of ignoring his mate's shrill warning and climbing in among the friendly stems. Abruptly, Imatuk rose up treading water and shrieking her alarm. Lutra flung backward and was at her side when other cries sounded. These came from the outer edge of the kelp field, where several of their number appeared to be caught fast. They were struggling, but could neither climb upon the kelp nor retreat to the water and the air was filled with their cries of consternation and terror.

What held them was a fiber net, concealed in sub-merged stems at the floe's outer edge, with meshes just large enough for otter heads to press through, but too tight to allow them to withdraw. Those not caught in the net were in great distress for the others, and their cries were as loud. Two more of the band blundered forward and were also caught.

Clutching her young one, Imatuk retreated seaward. Lutra and the others remained in the water below the nets crying with the caught ones until their voices grew faint and their struggles ceased. Still lamenting, they hung about, until in the early dark a dread sound, the slap and drip of paddles, drove them away.

The Spearing Surround

Far out beyond the kelp bed where the band had stopped, a ship lay at anchor. It had come in the night. Sitting up-reared at the edge of the floe, Lutra had sensed the vibration of its engines through the water. He did not know what it meant but in the last year or two he had come to recognize the sound as dangerous. Now they must move again and find a place to hide.

Lutra continued to stand guard until the first light, when the band began to stir, then he moved among them as he had learned to do, remembering in a kind of dream the low, alluring signals the elders of his early life used to make, less a command than a gentle voicing of the desire of all. The first to react were the nearest males, his own grown offspring among them. They repeated it, sounds no louder than a murmur, yet somehow rousing as a cheer. Suddenly, all were responding and acting together.

All but Imatuk: she was slow to come out of the tangle of kelp stems where she had slept, and now she dropped down at the edge of the field, looking about her in a kind of vague way, as if there were no urgency at all.

This slowness and vagueness of Imatuk's had begun some time ago after her pup was weaned, a gradual change from nervousness and fear to a state of unheeding dullness. Perhaps with the enemy everywhere and terror constant she had given up her vigilance in despair. In any case her watching and her warnings ceased. Lutra could no longer depend on his mate's nervous promptings, yet more and more he was looked to for guidance by the band.

In a sea otter clan there were no laws or rules to spoil a creature's fun. Leadership was a sort of happenstance, the magic of certain wise elders in making known things needed and wanted by all. In the past Lutra had never sensed that he was being led along the fine free ways of life. Yet guidance there must have been, for after the elders were gone there had been a sense of loss and confusion.

Lutra had learned vigilance from his over-anxious mate, but it was not Imatuk's sick fears which drove him. It was a growing sense of responsibility for his kind. As their numbers dwindled and the threat of extinction pressed in upon him, his wariness increased. Now it was Lutra who tested every water sound and sifted every breeze. It was he who sensed the time to go and signaled each change of direction, each stopping place along the way.

The band was keyed for flight, some already in the water, but Lutra had dropped down beside Imatuk. He was pressing against her side, gently nudging her with muzzle and shoulder. His followers looked on, confused by the delay.

Slowly Imatuk's wandering gaze focused upon Lutra and her low plaint quieted. He bumped her shoulder again,

swung his head playfully and moved toward the water looking back. She followed.

The band was in the water now, swimming in close
formation, face downward, dipping under the waves. For a
time Imatuk kept up. When she began to lag, Lutra tried to
put into his calls the promise of delicate feeding and safe
rest, but what he felt was the pressure of imminent danger.
Somehow a stark threat hung over these waters.

Imatuk seemed attentive again. Lutra signaled for
greater speed and the band was with him. Intent on escaping the unknown menace, he forgot her for a time. When
he looked for his mate she was far in their wake. He
glimpsed her white head at the top of a swell.

Lutra could not turn back or all would turn with him.
When he slowed, the band milled about him in confusion,
frustrated cries sounding. Apparently all felt the keen sense
of danger which drove him. He slowed them down as much
as he could, and Imatuk came on.

The band was moving together at its best travel speed,
but the delays had been costly. Somehow the enemy was
watching, coming closer. Suddenly there was a sound, a
kind of beat through the waters. The steadiness, the rhythm
of it was almost like that of killer whales coming in a line,
yet even more terrifying because they did not know what it
was. Imatuk must have heard it too for her speed had doubled. She was swimming beside Lutra, almost in the old
way.

The beat increased until it filled all the sea, then it
stopped. Moments later there was another sound that they
knew, though this time magnified—the slap and dip of
paddles. Lutra treaded water for a look. Still a good way
off, but it was the Great Enemy, this time a canoe with a
long tail.

It was the maneuver known as "the spearing surround." Dozens of bidarkas had been brought in by ship, ready with their Aleut paddlers to be lowered overside where sea otters were known to exist. There were sixty of the small narrow craft moving in a long line toward a point where otters had been sighted through a glass. Naturally the animals would submerge at their approach and remain so until the need for air forced them to the surface. The first animal to rise would be their cue. A single bidarka would paddle to the spot where the otter had disappeared again and station itself there, while the other canoes spread out in a wide circle. When the otters began to reappear a clamorous confusion of noise would be set up to make the animals dive quickly before they had had time to reoxidize their lungs, thus shortening their stay below the surface. The purpose also was to drive the otters toward the center of the circle of canoes where expert spearmen waited. Usually an entire band could be exterminated in this way.

From underwater Lutra saw the bottom of the central canoe, also its shadow with two upright figures in the slant of morning sun. He swerved without surfacing and swam deeper. Many of the band were still about him and did as he did, though the need for air was beginning to press on all. Swimming east, there were more canoe shadows with upright figures. Lutra swerved, shooting northward at an angle—more shadows there, many of them. The canoes were all around. Lutra doubled back, holding his breath to the bursting point. Then he had to surface, choosing a point where there were neither shadows nor canoe bottoms. Before he could more than snatch a breath a terrible din broke out from everywhere around, including those crashing reports which brought death.

Lutra and those around him dove again, descending to

the very bottom. Already breath was running out and some of them were driven to the surface. Lutra held on. Here on the bottom he could not hear the terrifying noise which was waiting for those who surfaced and driving them back almost at once, denied as before reoxidization in the life-giving air.

For a moment, terror and panic overwhelmed Lutra, for the enemy was holding them below until the agonizing need for air drove them up to be killed. Nearby was an outcrop of rock like a submerged reef full of holes and crevices. He clung to the weedy mass, holding himself down. If he pressed into one of the narrow crannies the rocks would hold him till he drowned. Better to expire down here than to face the bloody end that waited above. Voluntary death was not an unknown choice of his kind.

But the habit of acting for the clan was stronger. Those around him now would do as he did. Lutra swam upward watching for canoe shadows on the water, again choosing an area where none showed. Others of the band were about him as he surfaced and saw as he did the enemy at his work: as suffocating sea otters rose for breath, spears transfixed them and their bleeding bodies were lifted into the canoes. Blood was black on the water and the air Lutra gasped into his lungs had the smell of death. He prolonged their surface stay till the final instant, when two of the canoes were closing in. Then Lutra dove and the others with him.

They had breathed for an extra moment or two and so stayed down longer, clustered together in horror at what they had seen. Twice Lutra swam toward the encircling canoes, intent on escaping under and beyond, but wild crashing sounds drove him back. When they rose for a breath three canoes slid swiftly toward them, spearmen ready. Down again to the bottom rocks.

A snatched breath, long painful stays below; this went on and on, for the enemy seemed determined to have them all in the end. Once, swimming low over submerged rocks, Lutra caught sight of a wavering form partially hidden in a narrow rock cranny. The limp body swayed lifelessly with the current. He dove closer, and there was the white head of his mate held fast in a crevice of rock. Imatuk had chosen to die in the friendly sea and had deliberately wedged her body between two rocks, where not even her own final struggles could dislodge her.

She had been a beautiful, wise and worshipful mate, close as his own shadow in play and in danger, and Lutra would never take another. He stayed close beside her until his straining lungs forced him upward again.

It became impossible to catch a breath in that closing circle. The noise of the enemy was greater than ever— shouts, yells and a mighty slapping on the surface, all to confound and drive the last of the otter band to the center, where the killing was going on. Lutra and those few still with him could no longer see those tell-tale shadows on the water, only the churnings and widening circles of the beaten surface. But they had been pointed north and they kept going, braving in sheer desperation the cries and the churned waters above, defying their own paralyzing fears. They could not risk surfacing to breathe but they could swim on until they drowned, and so cheat the butchers as Imatuk had done.

On and on past all endurance. They were still swimming in deep water when the surface cleared and quieted. Lutra did not trust it even then, but pressed on until he and those with him simply popped upward for very life's sake. Then they lay on their backs with only their noses above water and breathed and breathed. Soon they were swimming again, more powerfully now with hope returned, and close beside Lutra, as they continued northward, was the round, white head of his son.

There were more dangers to meet with his small remaining band, many vicissitudes to face in the days that followed before Lutra's heightened instinct led them to a region of low-lying islands just south of the Alaskan Peninsula, the Sanak Islands. Here storms were born in the perennial mists that never wholly lifted. Besides being open to the whole expanse of the stormy North Pacific, the Sanaks were surrounded by a barricade of dangerous reefs, through which no ship could pass, not even a native *bidarka*. But stormy weather the sea otters loved and cold they could endure in their magnificent coats. Here they stayed.

There was another reason why whole seasons passed with no sign of the enemy. Something wonderful had happened out in the world. It had finally been recognized in several lands that the sea otter was very nearly extinct, and legislation had been passed making it a prison offense to kill a sea otter anywhere from California to the Bering Sea.

The longer they stayed here, the more they took on the wild free spirit of the place. Breeding began again and pups were born. Happy families sported in the surf and fed on the shellfish clustered among the tidal rocks. When restlessness took them there were other nearby islets to swim to, all of them their own, shared only by sea birds. Their island home, rock-solid and never invaded, they had found at last.